C000171775

## BRITAIN IN OLD PH

# THE LAKE COUNTIES AT WORK

*J O H N   M A R S H*

ALAN SUTTON PUBLISHING LIMITED

Alan Sutton Publishing Limited
Phoenix Mill · Far Thrupp · Stroud
Gloucestershire · GL5 2BU

First published 1995

*Title page photograph*: The porter poses
outside the King's Arms Hotel, Kendal.
*Cover photographs*: A timber wagon in trouble,
and a worker bringing down slate from
Honister.

**British Library Cataloguing in Publication Data.**
A catalogue record for this book is available from
the British Library.

ISBN 0-7509-0888-2

Typeset in 9/10 Sabon.
Typesetting and origination by
Alan Sutton Publishing Limited.
Printed in Great Britain by
Ebenezer Baylis, Worcester.

This book is dedicated to my wife Jean who helps me
in my hobby in many ways.

Haymaking at Ambleside.

# Contents

The Prince of Wales, Grasmere, with the Riggs' Windermere to Keswick coach at the coach entrance. This was one of the most popular tourist routes but Riggs, as well as catering for tourists, ran a regular service throughout the year and advertised as Royal Mail Coaches – possibly the last in the country – until motor transport changed everything. Here coachman Terry Fiddler can be seen with 'his flea-bitten greys' in the early years of the twentieth century.

# Introduction

Cumberland, Westmorland and Lancashire North of the Sands are the old county areas included in this collection. On All Fools' Day 1974 they were amalgamated into the modern county of Cumbria where, to the annoyance of some, they have remained ever since. The ancient name Cumbria, predating the Normans who were responsible for many of the boundaries which lasted from their day up to the 1974 changes, is probably as appropriate a name for this corner of England as any, but this book uses another – *The Lake Counties* – a title which came into use with the Romantic Movement from the eighteenth century. The County Borough of Barrow-in-Furness and the City of Carlisle are within the geographical area but should not, by definition, be included. Nevertheless pictures from within their boundaries are included to balance the whole. Both towns deserve books of their own.

I grew up in Furness when the sky was lit by night with the iron and steel works of Ulverston, Barrow and Millom; huge ships were manufactured at Barrow; the ghosts of the Furness iron industry and the Coniston copper mining were more obvious than today and there seemed to be railway tracks everywhere. My friends and I, as boys, visited auction marts to listen to the local dialect and probably rubbed shoulders with Beatrix Potter. We rowed on Coniston when Arthur Ransome was fishing there, but we did not know if we crossed his path as we adventured over countryside which now is featured in travel brochures but then was mostly a working landscape. Did the mines and quarries go right through the mountain at Coniston? We tried to find out. How long does it take to row the length of Windermere and Coniston lakes? Royalty was observed from afar as it came to the district, sometimes to launch ships, at other times to stay with the local gentry and make visits to places where the local children, issued with Union Jack flags, were permitted to view the goings-on.

I have worked all my working life in the 'Lake Counties', as have many generations of my ancestors, but I can still find the scenery exciting. The history of the district is doubly interesting as, until fairly recent times, a great deal was conjecture because so little was written down.

It is the 'working' parts of the Lake Counties this book attempts to capture, although the beauty of the land must also be seen – how can it be avoided? – even though it was much exploited, as were many of the workers. I have also included a section on the travel industry which now employs so many and which is directly related to 'Lakeland'. I have used many photographs of the Pepper family and its descendants. They illustrate, as well as any might, the Lakeland 'worker' family: proud, hard-working, God-fearing, and farming a tenanted small-holding as well as doing another job, in their case mining and quarrying. The advent of the Langdale linen industry was also within this family, whose women were involved in 'Arts and Crafts' for four generations.

The photographs cover the period from the late nineteenth century into the middle of the twentieth, but they can only illustrate parts of the wide and diverse geographical spread of working life. At the turn of the century times were bad for all but a very few, and the introduction of the old-age pension by the Liberal government in 1908 only helped a little. Real poverty continued to be a problem until well after the Second World War. The stress of working life can certainly be seen in the faces in some of the photographs.

I have included, where possible, the name of the photographer with the pictures. These were the workers without whose labours this book would not have been possible. Before 1850 there were no photographers. Through the 1870s and '80s photographic businesses arrived in every town, and from the 1890s popular pictures were available for many uses; in particular, as the century changed, the picture postcard. I have included both picture postcards and pictures from private family albums.

In recent decades various societies and working groups have started to investigate the working life of the Lake Counties which, amazingly, stretches back to the Stone Age when Langdale had a large manufactory for stone axes. The economic history of the counties has, after all, affected, more than anything else, the scenery and society of the district; the farming and its markets; the mining and its transport; the quarrying and its often dire consequences on the landscape; the boat-building and the harbours. The holiday trade and its hotels and 'facilities'; and, of course, the working people, sometimes imported, whose humble cottages are now in great demand as holiday homes, and the entrepreneurs who built large houses, many now hotels, and bought land to make estates.

Much modern research into working Cumbria is related, in one way or another, to the Cumberland and Westmorland Antiquarian and Archaeological Society. This society was founded in 1866 and ever since has been the centre of recorded Cumbrian history. Its influence has been broad in a county lacking a university and hardly able to afford the museums situated within its boundaries. Modern theses, articles and books now relate the story of past industrial and 'working' experience. Many of the authors were, as I am, members of the 'C & W' – indeed, anyone claiming to have a serious interest in the history of the Lake Counties can hardly miss being a member. Oral history groups also record the thoughts of many working people.

My book draws on these many sources but does not claim to be anything other than a nostalgic illustrated introduction to what working people did in the fairly recent past, just on the borderline of living memory. If these pictures prompt anyone to take a closer look at the whole subject of working Cumbria or a more detailed study of any part of the wide range of activities depicted the book has more than served its purpose.

John Marsh
Spring 1995

*Section One*

# THE FARMING
# SCENE

*'Miss Daisy Briggs and her fowls' was the title of
this photograph by M. Groocock when it appeared
in Mackereth's Year Book of 1900. Miles Hugh
Groocock was one of Ulverston's early photographers, with premises at 5 Hart Street. He also
advertised gas for sale for lantern lectures.
William Briggs was a grocer and seedsman of
13 Market Street, Ulverston (he lived at
2 Princes Street).*

Haymaking was a common sight a hundred years ago and here Matthew Walling of Dawson Fold Farm, Lyth, is pictured in the field with his haycart, ready to lead the horse back to the farm. The Walling family have been at Dawson Fold since the middle of the nineteenth century and are to be found all over Crosthwaite and Lyth parish today.

'Looking to the horse' at Seatoller, Borrowdale, photographed by the Alfred Pettitt of Keswick studio in the early twentieth century. Fell farmers used their horses to get about on the high fells, as well as for pulling the sled trailers on which they recovered injured sheep and collected stone, bracken and hay. The same horse would take the carriage into Keswick on market-day. Many tales persist of horses on some farms receiving better treatment than the human beings.

Dalton Hall, near Burton in Kendal, is on what was the Lancashire/Westmorland border. Joseph Moorhouse was the head gardener to Edmund Geoffrey Stanley Hornby, 'the squire', when this photograph was taken of the extensive walled garden situated next to Home Farm at Dalton Hall. Up to the 1960s exotic fruit was grown in the extensive heated greenhouses against the south-facing wall. The neatness of the scene on this Rowbotham of Burton picture points a sad contrast with today.

The Herdwick sheep of Lakeland are famous and the local photographers used them to increase their sales to visitors. Here Henry Mayson of Keswick caught a terrier-type sheepdog with a flock of sheep 'changing pasture' near Lodore at the end of the nineteenth century.

Mr B. Wilson of Sand Gap Farm bought mangold seed from W.H. Mackereth, Market Place, Ulverston. The resulting harvest of mangolds was photographed by W. Holmes, photographer, of Lightburn Road, Ulverston, for the *1897 Year Book*. 'As big as my head', for the little lad at the back.

The crossing of a Border Leicester ram with a local Herdwick ewe was a great success for William T. Lawrence, the farm manager at the Cumberland County Council farm at Newton Rigg, Penrith, here photographed with his half-bred ewe, 1912. 'Lambs fatten early, when put on turnips and given a little corn. 40 to 50 shillings is the usual selling price when they are fat at the nearest auction.'

Bull breeding for export is demonstrated with Mr J.K. Shephard's shorthorn bull 'Lord Nelson'. After taking first prize in 1903 at Whitehaven, Barrow, Gosforth and Millom shows the bull was sold to Buenos Aires for breeding in Argentina's huge fatstock and meat-canning trade.

A pastoral scene on Derwentwater, from the studio of Henry Mayson of Keswick. Henry Mayson set up his photographic studio in Lake Road, Keswick, in the 1880s, almost next door to the Abrahams. The fierce competition between the Keswick 'big three' photographers, Abraham, Mayson and Pettitt, is a story on its own. The sheep, cows and horses of the local farmers featured on many of the pictures sold by all three.

Fostering 'pet' lambs took a twist at John Hutchinson's farm at Holeslack, Helsington, Kendal, when Meg the sheepdog assumed some of the task, c. 1905. Photographer Thomas James Ewan, who was also a postman, of Yard 67, Stricklandgate, Kendal, took a number of pictures to record the events.

Farmers frequently had a milk round to supplement their farming income: here the dairy cart of Richard Bell of Helsfell Farm near Kendal is seen on its round at Castle Crescent, Kendal, at the beginning of the twentieth century. The milk went straight from the churn into the jug.

Breeding racehorses was the occupation of Mr Boardman of Thornleigh, near Burton in Kendal, and here the horses make their highly strung way on exercise through the main street of the village. Note the unmade carriageway and cobbled footpaths.

In the wild Cumberland borderlands with Scotland the horse was often the only way that any distance could be covered. Here a young Joseph Lauder is seen astride his good-looking horse at the Dog and Gun Inn at Bailey, near Bewcastle.

'Lakeland Shepherd' by Abrahams became a famous photograph in its day, selling on many hundreds of postcards. Note that, unlike the rider on the last picture, the shepherd does not use a saddle. The sentimentality implied with horse, man, sheep and dog in these pictures obscures the harsh truth of the hard life for all four (see also page 23).

Burton, Milnthorpe and Carnforth Agricultural Society's annual show was held at Milnthorpe, 26 August 1926. 'Beautiful weather', reported the *Westmorland Gazette*. Mr Newhaven, with a 'very promising youngster', won first prize in the foal class, while Mrs Halhead and her sons presented 'a useful animal which stood well with magnificent quarters and a good mane', which won the carthorse foal class.

The rebuilding of Hodge Hill farm buildings at Cartmel Fell was carried out by builder John Kellett of Lound Cottage (he was also a county councillor and served as a school manager, as well as being the agent for the Atlas Assurance Company), John William Fleming of Chapel House (and later Swallowmire), the carter and joiner Robert Leighton Matthews of Haycote Steam Saw Mill, Crosthwaite with assistants M. Dewhurst and J. King. Here they are seen with their workmen posing 'on the job'.

A task for winter at every Lakeland farm was the sawing of sufficient logs to last through to spring. Here Robert Fell of Holme Ground, Tilberthwaite, near Coniston, is seen at work with either a neighbour or a paying visitor to the farm helping with the task. From the late nineteenth century as the tourist trade developed many farmers took in bed-and-breakfast tourists to supplement their income. Some of the tourists found farm chores novel fun and gladly lent a hand.

Harvest Festival was a time for decorating the church, and all the local farming families took part. In the smaller communities harvest time was a major social event. Here we see Little Asby Congregational Chapel decorated for the 1897 harvest, when the Revd Joseph Cockram was at the manse.

Another Harvest Festival in a village church was the September 1907 event at Spark Bridge Wesleyan Chapel. 'It is our harvest festival we had a few Sundays ago. The place was crowded out,' says the postcard. Christmas, Easter and Harvest were the three occasions when most villagers went to their local church or chapel.

Hiring fairs for farm labourers included entertainment in the form of touring roundabouts, swings, etc. Emerson and Hazard toured in the Lake Counties and their fairground ride, 'three abreast jumpers', is seen here at Dalton-in-Furness. The engine 'Lightning II' can just be seen in the background (see page 63). The hirings died out between the wars but the entertainment continues to tour the county today.

'Charms of Kirkby Lonsdale' was a typical postcard produced with a view to sales to both holidaymakers and locals. Raphael Tuck's oilette, 'Country Courtship', shows two women at work with a suitor for both on hand. Before the First World War this type of picture was in great demand. It had little to do with the back-breaking manual grind of harvest time.

Thomas Nelson of Holme Ground, Tilberthwaite, Coniston, is seen here with his bull, Tim Tossett, and farm dog, Jack, *c.* 1922. His son Louis James Lancaster Nelson takes a tentative hold of the end of the bull rope. Young Louis Nelson later went into the garage trade. A daughter, Abigail, followed a very different 'trade' (see page 109).

Holme Ground, Tilberthwaite, is again shown here with Robert Pepper, two generations earlier, shepherding sheep into the yard. His wife Elizabeth was, with her mother, very active in the famous Langdale linen industry started by John Ruskin in the late nineteenth century. Their house, built to house a quarry manager for the local slate quarries, was bought by Beatrix Potter and is now owned by the National Trust. Branches of the same family have occupied the house through to our time; they have been tenant farmers and quarrymen as well as being at the centre of Langdale linen.

Mrs Akister of Little Ream, Ulverston, 'in her well-known turn-out', *c.* 1900. Local farming families used locally made carts such as this for most of their transport needs. Mrs Akister's husband Aaron's farm transport was apparently Mrs Akister's task. Here the pair of them are seen with their cart and piebald pony.

Dowthwaite's 6 hp McLaren traction engine (number 1015) and thresher seen outside Dan Clark's butcher's shop, Penrith, *c.* 1910. H. Dowthwaite and Sons, Skelton, Penrith, became the local supplier of steam-powered road and farm engines, and had a contract with Cumberland County Council for steamrollers. William Dowthwaite, famous for his high standards, retired in 1970 and sold the business.

Shearing a sheep at Satterthwaite, near Hawkshead, photographed by B. Coward of Satterthwaite, 1930s. In the first decades of the twentieth century Satterthwaite's inhabitants were mostly concerned with the wood industry or with Force Forge. Many were woodcutters – see pages 33 and 34 – and some were farmers.

'The shepherd's pets.' Another of the pictures from Abraham of Keswick's studio which frankly glamorized the wool and mutton trade of the high fell area. Fell farming sheep was, and still is, hard, wet and dirty work with little reward generally (see also page 16).

All the family joined in the back-breaking labour at haytime at Natland Mill Beck (or Millbeck) Farm, near Kendal, 1930s. John Dixon Chapman and his wife Isabella were members of the family which had been at this farm since the mid-nineteenth century. The many developments which have been allowed all round this farm in recent decades have changed the once-rural area for ever, as nearby Kendal gobbles up the surrounding countryside.

At Old College, Windermere, the fee-paying pupils were roped in to assist with the haymaking. This was advertised in the prospectus under 'Odd Jobs': 'The boys give a hand towards turning the hay in their playtime; and when it is ready for leading we get to work by noon, having lunch and tea in the field, small boys with a rope apiece are as useful as the orthodox cart, and much more amusing.' The last load for the evening came in on a cart pulled by Mrs Raike's trap pony. Character-building or exploitation – the line was thin (see also page 113).

Robert and Mary Fell, quarryman and lacemaker. Robert Fell succeeded the Nelsons at Holme Ground (see page 21) with his wife Mary Pepper, after first being at Tilberthwaite Farm. Quarry work saw the end of Robert at sixty-three years of age after a terrible accident at Tunnel Hole Quarry, Coniston, in 1938. Mary was the daughter of Robert and Elizabeth Pepper of Holme Ground, and she carried on her mother's interest in lacemaking and spinning.

Two photographs of the Blencathra pack of foxhounds. The top picture shows the October 1934 meet at Caldbeck, the burial place of the famous hunter John Peel, who died in 1854. John Peel's great-great-grandson can be seen in a trilby second from the left. In the lower picture Maysons of Keswick record a meet at about the same time at the Borrowdale Hotel, near Keswick. A regular visit by the local pack of foxhounds was (and is) essential for the well-being of any fell farm.

Elizabeth Mary Abigail Fell, daughter of Mary and Robert Fell, poses at the spinning wheel in the dying days of the Langdale linen industry. Elizabeth was attempting to learn the skills of her great-grandmother, grandmother, mother and aunts, but as the years surrounding the First World War went by the economic base of the 'industry' collapsed, leaving the skills as a hobby for future generations.

The Wilson Estate at Rigmaden in the Lune Valley had a number of farms bought by the family over many years and rented out to tenant farmers. In the top picture the continuing task of wood clearance 'logging' is seen at Haggwood. A contrast can be seen in the lower picture where, instead of the straightforward lift on the Wilson Estate, another group of woodmen at Greenodd attempt to lift tree-trunks out of a field on to a waggon on a higher road. Logging was never easy, as the cover picture and the heavy log on the road of the Greenodd picture confirm. Many prosecutions can be read in late nineteenth-century local newspapers for cruelty to the horses in the log trade.

A woodland trade associated with many nineteenth-century and earlier industries was the provision of basket 'swills'. These were used to carry anything from washing to coal and bobbins as well as farm animal feed – anything where a basket would be useful. Here two lots of swill-makers from the High Furness area can be seen in the first decade of the twentieth century. The lower picture is by James Atkinson of Ulverston.

The Bobbin Mill at Skelwith Bridge was that of Jackson Coward. The Cowards of Skelwith Bridge had featured in the forming of the Langdale linen industry when they manufactured spinning-wheels, using the remains of ancient machines as patterns. 'At Skelwith Bridge lived a clever carpenter and bobbin turner,' said Hardwicke Rawnsley in 1901, 'and incited to the task by the enthusiasm of the wheel finders and "fettlers", and with such suggestions as the dames who had spun when they were children could supply, the bobbin maker Coward contrived to make twelve new wheels.'

One industry where baskets were used was the bobbin industry. This photograph shows
the 'blocking machine' at 'Mr Phillipson's Bobbin Works at Spark Bridge'. Overleaf the
roughing machine is depicted.

The roughing machine with its juvenile minder clearly shows a swill being used. Both this picture and the one on the previous page date from 1899. This type of primitive machinery can still be seen today in the Stott Park Bobbin Mill, Finsthwaite, where a remarkable museum has been formed, now owned by English Heritage, and in which a lost way of life has been preserved.

Two views of work in the woods of High Furness. In the top picture Herbert Bell of Ambleside captures a group of three charcoal burners having their lunch. Below, another group poses with their fire almost made. One result of this activity was the coppicing of huge tracts of woodland on a rotation basis, which produced a southern Lake District landscape very different from today's leafy glades.

The charcoal burners and other woodland workers made themselves distinctive wigwam-type huts of branches covered in turf in which they, and sometimes their families, lived while they were about their woodland tasks. Here photographer W. Holmes of Ulverston pictures a group in the Furness woods with their hut and tools in around 1905.

# Section Two

# INDUSTRY

The great industrial area of Barrow-in-Furness was a county borough of the old county of Lancashire. Its iron and steel manufacture and its ship-building are part of the story of a few entrepreneurs who combined in the nineteenth century to change the landscape and economy of the Furness peninsula. Valentine's of Dundee recorded some of the work. Here is the boilermakers' shop at the Vickers Shipyard.

The platers' shed (above) and the steel foundry (below) are two more views taken by Valentine's at the height of the boom in shipbuilding and steel working. Self-sufficiency was obvious in the amazing Vickers works as warships and submarines, liners and cargo ships were manufactured for Britain and countries all over the world. Circumstances have now reduced the yard to a shadow of its former glory.

Workers at Barrow came from all over the world – particularly in wartime. Here an Australian ammunition worker had his photograph taken during the First World War for his family and friends, 'With kind regards from Charlie to Jack, 26.1.16 Australian Munition Worker, Vickers Ltd., Barrow, England', is written on the back of the picture.

The huge iron ore mines, together with the associated ironworks (see opposite) attracted labour from a wide area and resulted in a new town being built adjacent to an ancient castle and church at Millom. Here a group of miners at the Hodbarrow mine is photographed for the family album. The miner in the middle of the front row is young Robert Fell, later to live at Holme Ground, Tilberthwaite (see pages 25 and 50). Note the candles stuck to the men's helmets.

The Coniston mountains were exploited for their copper as well as quarried for their slate. Here part of the works can be seen in the late nineteenth century when worked by the Coniston Mining Company, when Mr B. Johns was manager and secretary. The Furness Railway 9-mile-long branch line from Foxfield was extended in 1860 beyond Coniston station to the Coppermines Wharf. The extensive mines not only produced copper but included iron ore, lead, blende and nickel in their mineral range. In 1882 it was reported that the mine had thirteen waterwheels for power and fifty hands were employed.

The Millom Iron Works was one of a series from Carnforth in Lancashire along the coast all the way up to Workington. Local outcrops of iron ore were worked initially. The Millom and Askam Haematite and Steel Company had John Graham as secretary at the turn of the century when they had six furnaces and employed six hundred men. Illingworth's of Millom photographed their works, *c.* 1905.

The Kendal Gasworks, situated in Gas House Lane (now Parkside Road) and built against the Lancaster to Kendal Canal, is now no more. Its demise corresponded with the closing of other gasworks as natural gas took over from its manufactured cousin. The Kendal works were started by the Kendal Fell Trust as 'The Kendal Gas Light and Coke Company' as part of their brief to light the town in 1825. The supply of water was included in a new company in 1846 and all was later combined with the provision of electricity under the Kendal Borough Council. Traces of both the early gasworks and the later electricity works can still be seen at the site.

The Moss Bay works at Workington at the turn of the century was only part of the huge industrial area around this ancient seaside town. 'The Moss Bay Haematite Iron and Steel Co. Ltd, the Workington Haematite Iron & Steel Co. Ltd, Kirk Bros & Co., the Lowther Haematite Iron Co. Ltd, Cammel & Co. Ltd and the Distington Haematite Co. Ltd all have important works here,' says *Kelly's Directory*. Two pictures show parts of the Moss Bay complex. The postcard in the top picture gives the information, 'Father is the keeper of the furnace with the X on it.'

Moss Bay works at night are seen in the top picture. Postcard producers took many photographs such as this at Ulverston, Barrow, Askham and Millom as well as at Workington. Posted in May 1903 the postcard attempts to illustrate the amazing pyrotechnic-like night skies then almost taken for granted along the Cumberland and north Lancashire coast. In the postcard below, by Debenham's of 158 Pow Street, Workington, King George V and Queen Mary with their wartime entourage are pictured on their visit there, May 1917. 'The Royal party on the Pig Beds, Moss Bay' is the title of the picture.

The Buttermere Greenslate quarries at Honister, showing slate being sledded down the scree. This was when Moses Pepper of Seatoller House, Borrowdale, was the manager (see page 97). Speaking of Buttermere parish, *Bulmer's Directory* says, 'the greater portion of the land is devoted to sheep pasture and in attending the flocks which range the hills the people find their employment; a few however work in the Slate Quarries of Honister Crag, which forms the south bank of the narrow vale of Gatescarthdale'.

Said to be the last female coal miner in Whitehaven, Sal Madge has recently had her story told in a Whitehaven Museum booklet by Ray Devlin. Sarah Madgin (1831–99) apparently did not work down the pits 'as legend tells but as a carter in Croft Pit yard, and was a football player and wrestler. 'She dearly loved her "chew of baccy" and drank beer by the pint,' says Devlin; she also 'possessed a kindly heart'. In 1993 the Friends of Whitehaven Museum had a headstone erected on the pauper's grave of this famous Whitehaven character. 'Very few women will have had such an arduous life. She is and always will remain a part of the history of Whitehaven,' reads her dedication.

Many small foundry workshops were run in towns throughout Lakeland. A busy foundry for many years was Day's of Canal Head, Kendal, seen here at the turn of the century. In the top picture is the 'mould for large Bedplate; put together in several parts', and below is one of their 'fire ranges', once so common throughout south Lakeland, during the process of manufacture. Set up near the Canal Head Ironworks of Gilbert Gilkes, Harold H. Day's Castle Foundry was a very busy local works until closure in 1938 when it was taken over by Gilkes.

K Shoes is now a famous trading name but it started life as the shoe factory of Somervell Bros, who had the letter K imprinted into their leather to prevent theft by employees. Here Jack Simon is seen with the sole press at K Shoes' factory, *c.* 1900.

The K Shoes' works on the banks over the River Kent at Kendal has expanded over the many decades since it was sited on the riverside near the Nether Bridge in 1844. Here reproduced is one of their trade cards from the years between the two world wars, showing the manufacture of the then famous K boot as well as the despatch warehouse and the works on the riverside. Recent years of foreign competition and takeover have not been kind to this large Kendal employer.

Working stone has long been the trade of many workers in Lakeland. It is a wet, cold and dirty job with little pay. Here two pictures show stone-breaking (for road stone) in a Furness quarry, *c.* 1900, pictured by James Atkinson of Ulverston. William Nevinson is seen in the lower picture slate splitting at Horse Crag Quarry, Tilberthwaite, 1930. At least William had a shelter from the rain. He walked from Little Langdale to earn his pay.

Greenside Lead Ore Mine, Glenridding, Patterdale, had been in operation for 150 years when this picture, from the first decade of the twentieth century, was taken. William Henry Borlase of Greenside Lodge was the mining engineer at the time, as well as being a parish and rural district councillor. His mine was the first in England to use electrical power for haulage after many years of using electricity for other purposes. Pneumatic drilling eased the lot of the miners working the very hard rock. This mine throughout the nineteenth century, and well into the twentieth, was very successful indeed, even selling the silver from the ore to the Bank of England. At the time of the picture John Comer of Glenridding Cottage was mine agent as well as being a churchwarden. Other agents in the village were William Mitchell of Eagle House and Joseph Shaw of 3 Stybarrow Terrace. Matthew Place of Brown House was the secretary to the Fernside Lead Mining Company.

Thrang Quarry, Langdale, was visited by Raphael Tuck, who produced a set of postcards for visitors to the area. Here rockhands are pictured about their dangerous task long before Health and Safety at Work had even been considered. This was again a wet and dirty job for poor pay, but with the chance to appear on the postcard stands at the souvenir shops at Chapel Stile and Skelwith Bridge.

Quarrying at Pink Rock Quarry, Shap (above), was just as hard, wet and dirty. The picture card was used by the Shap Granite Co. Ltd, as an acknowledgement of an order, with the printed proviso, 'Deliveries are subject to conditions of weather, wagon supply, unforeseen circumstances, Strikes, Lock-outs, Acts of God that might limit or stop production. Telegrams "Felspar Shap". Telephone Shap 5.' The lower picture, by S.G. Lamb of Millom, shows Kirkby Moor quarry workers in the late nineteenth century. Robert Fell from Tilberthwaite (see pages 25 and 38), is third from the left in the back row.

Lamb Hill Quarry, Moresby, was photographed by a quarryman for his family album. The workmen in the top picture pose alongside one of the tripod and boom cranes. In the lower picture the working sheds where the rough stone was worked into squared-off blocks can clearly be seen on the right. Tom McKay and Son of Main Street, St Bees and Aspatria, had quarries at Sandwith and Lamb Hill, Parton, Moresby, in the years leading up to the Second World War.

Gunpowder was an important trade for many years with the ample supplies of water and charcoal assisting manufacture. The great Elterwater Gunpowder Works founded in Langdale in 1824 was transformed into a holiday park in the 1930s. Here (above) workers pose with boxes of their sticks of compressed explosive in the late nineteenth century for photographer M. Davies of Millom. Below, coopers, who made casks for the storage and transport of gunpowder, are photographed by James Atkinson of Ulverston at the end of the nineteenth century.

# RAIL, ROAD AND WATER TRANSPORT

*The Midland Railway took its own route to Scotland via Leeds, building the most spectacular of the North–South routes in the process. Here Compound 4–4–0 number 997 approaches Carlisle with the 'Scotch Express'.*

Midland Railway 4–4–0 engine number 1000, just after takeover by the London Midland and Scottish Company in 1923, passing through Armathwaite station. 'Via the Midland section from St Pancras passing Sheffield, Leeds and Carlisle – 9 hours 10 minutes to Edinburgh and 9 hours 20 minutes to Glasgow,' states the card. (Euston to Glasgow and Edinburgh via Crewe and Preston was 8 hours 15 minutes.) This engine was built in 1902 as Midland Compound number 2631; it was rebuilt in 1907 and renumbered 1000. In 1951 it was retired from main line duty and was restored by British Railways as a preserved locomotive. Today it can be seen at York.

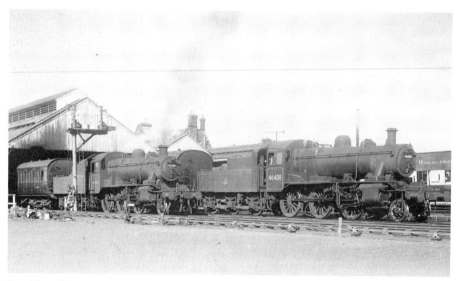

Penrith railway station on 5 August 1952 with Ivatt 'Mogul' 2–6–0 engines numbers 46448 and 46488 standing with passenger trains. These ex-LMS engines were frequently used on the Cockermouth, Keswick and Penrith branch line (see page 62). Penrith was the main line junction with lines to Workington via Keswick and Darlington via Kirkby Stephen – both no longer exist.

Tebay station, engine sheds, goods sidings and junction with the North Eastern Railway are no more. Trains now pass through here at speeds of around 100 miles per hour, and the background of this view is now the M6 motorway. What was once an important railway town has been forced to adopt different ways. Here, on 4 August 1954, the Manchester to Glasgow express pulled by Royal Scot 4–6–0 engine number 46121 (Highland Light Infantry, City of Glasgow Regiment) travels north while other engines work in the once-extensive sidings.

On the south coast of the Lake Counties at Kents Bank station, Furness Railway 0–6–0 Sharp Stewart locomotive number 85 is seen with a three-coach local passenger train at the turn of the century. In those days Kents Bank station had a stationmaster and staff. It survives today as an unstaffed halt.

The line from Hincaster junction on the London and North Western Railway and Arnside on the Furness Railway was opened on 26 June 1876. The reason for the route was to provide coal from the north-east to the industry of Barrow-in-Furness, and here such a train was photographed on the embankment from Dallam viaduct towards Sandside station with an ex-Maryport and Carlisle engine, used on the Tebay to Barrow coke trains from 1927. This line no longer exists.

Ulverston Canal was opened in 1796 and the railway between Carnforth and Ulverston was built over it in 1857. The opening of docks at Barrow and the coming of the railway sealed the fate of the shortest, deepest and widest canal in England. Here a goods train travels south towards Plumpton. In the background the chimneys of the Ulverston Ironworks can be seen.

Wetheral station 'on the Carlisle and Newcastle section of the North Eastern Railway' is pictured by Nicholson and Cartner of Carlisle before the First World War. A porter attends the arrival of a train. At the turn of the century Thomas Milburn was the stationmaster, and William Henry Brider, Alex Stewart and Robert Lowther were signalmen.

Cleator and Workington junction railway engine number 5 and Whitehaven Cleator and Egremont railway engine number 111, at Distington station in the nineteenth century. The engine crews and stationmaster pose for the picture: note the polished boots.

A Furness Railway goods train is seen near Grange-over-Sands in this photograph by the Locomotive Publishing Co., dating from before the First World War. Rebuilt Sharp Stewart 0–6–0 No. 97 pulls a set of extended top wagons.

'The Eskdale Express at Boot' is the title of this view on 'La'al Ratty' – the Eskdale railway from Ravenglass to Boot. Built originally in 3 ft gauge in 1882 as a mine railway the line was closed in 1913 to be rebuilt as a 15 in gauge miniature railway, which today attracts many tourists. Passengers were carried in the mine railway days in train sets such as these, pictured at the turn of the century.

Stainmore on the north-eastern route between Penrith and Darlington also carried coal trains for Furness via Tebay (see page 55). This line was often blocked with snow in winter, as here in 1955 near Kirkby Stephen. Train snowploughs also became stuck and the line frequently had to be cleared by men with spades – and then the engine boiler had to be thawed out.

The gunpowder works at Gatebeck had a connection with the main line at Milnthorpe by way of a horse tramline along the side of the Peasey Beck, across the canal at Crooklands by a bridge and then alongside the road into Milnthorpe station. For many years Wadeson Barrow was one of the drivers who took loads of explosives down the line. The maximum load was 4 tons 10 cwt. Wadeson is seen here, *c*. 1933.

Another horse tramway was that built on the old canal from Carlisle to Port Carlisle. The canal was cut from the harbour, built by Lord Lonsdale in 1819, to the city of Carlisle in 1823. The canal was filled in and a horse tramway laid along its length in 1854 to a junction with the North British Silloth to Carlisle railway at Drumburgh station. William Oliphant was the tramway stationmaster at the turn of the century.

Steam power was used on road vehicles for many years, and in the top photograph taken near Longtown the roadmen are seen with their steamroller, *c.* 1910. In the lower picture, pipes for the Manchester Corporation Waterworks pipeline are seen in Kendal railway station yard after being loaded on to Charlie Cumpstey's steam wagon, with driver Jack Kellett standing by the engine.

This Cockermouth, Keswick and Penrith Railway advertising appeared in the E.J. Burrow *Lake District Guide* from just after the First World War. The closing of this line and the 'improving' of the A66 trunk road through the Keswick Valley must be the most short-sighted and offensive of the recent planning policies inflicted on the central Lakes.

The Crosby Garrett stationmaster David Reynolds was very proud of his station house garden, as this turn of the century photograph confirms. The station, in a cutting on the Settle to Carlisle Midland line, exists no longer but it was said, in the nineteenth century, that the building of the station provided the isolated local population with an opportunity to travel which had previously not been possible.

The saving of traction engine 'Lightning II' from the scrap heap was due to the work of Bill Stables of Ulverston who acquired the Burrell 7 hp steam traction engine No. 3562 (reg. no. AO 6302) from Emerson and Hazard, the travelling fair, just after the Second World War when steam engines were being replaced by huge ex-WD diesel units. Here 'Lightning II' can be seen in its first resting-place after the fair – a piece of land off Neville Street, Ulverston. Even then the enthusiasts gathered to admire the mighty engine.

The arrival of Jeffries' travelling fair at Hillsbottom, Kirkby Stephen, in 1954 shows the sort of large diesel traction unit which had by then replaced the steam fairground engine. After the Second World War the original reason for many of the town fairs (the animal sales) had virtually disappeared but the entertainment continued to travel round the area in the time-honoured fashion.

Ernest Bennett's diesel-engined Leyland lorry is being used to take the load off a crashed steam goods vehicle which came to rest in front of Clark and Gibson's cycle shop at the top of Church Street, Ambleside. Oil-lamp lighting, hard tyres all round and hard luck for the cycle shop owner.

Clearing the Keswick to Kendal road looks doomed to failure as the snow starts to fall
again, March 1937. Blizzards halted rail and road transport and brought down many
telephone cables. The gales filled the road with snow-drifts, and Abrahams of Keswick
recorded the scene for posterity. One hundred and eighty bank managers at a
conference at the Keswick Hotel had an enforced extension to their visit because the
weather prevented them from leaving. The managers of Ambleside and Windermere
banks spent most of Sunday walking home to open their branches on the Monday.

The driver of this car was attempting to cross Dunmail Raise on the Keswick to Ambleside road when he was caught in the same snowstorms as shown in the last picture. He spent the whole of the night of Saturday 6 March in his motor car until rescued by, as the photograph says, 'A despised friend'. The 5.20 p.m. bus from Ambleside to Penrith got stuck on Dunmail until the following Monday, and the roadmen used it as a shelter.

Near Penrith golf course the Ribble Leyland service bus (reg. no. CK 4192) on the Penrith to Salkeld service had to be rescued from the drifts in the same March 1937 snowstorms. Nine months later the snow was again blocking roads and railway lines as winter started early.

Snow at the turn of the century at Cartmel Fell was cleared from the road in front of the vicarage by use of a horse-plough and manpower. The photograph dates from the time when the Revd Thomas Price MA lived in the vicarage, and Frederick Taylor the roadman lived at Strawberry Bank.

Two views of early transport trading. Above, Joseph Hewertson's garage at Beresford Road, Windermere, can be seen. Here one could hire cars, cycles or prams, the complete service for the holidaymaker. Below is E.J. Tiffen's cycle shop at Irishgate Brow, Carlisle. They manufactured 'Castle' brand cycles using BSA parts. In the 1905 *Carlisle Directory* Tiffens advertised 'Castle Specials' with two brakes and Dunlop tyres at £7 10s, and 'Coaster and two-speed hubs fitted to any make of machine'.

Armstrong and Fleming at Penrith were the Rolls-Royce agent in an affluent area. Here in the early 1920s mechanic Jack Pounder, who much later had a popular barber's shop in Penrith, poses with Rolls-Royce reg. no. EC 5475. Jack was also, with the author, a founding chorus member of the Penrith Savoyards when *The Mikado* was performed at Tynefield School, 6–11 February 1959. This picture brings happy memories of a man of many parts.

In Kendal Atkinson and Griffin had a garage at 58 Highgate, almost opposite the Town Hall. Talbot and Darracq cars and New Hudson cycles are advertised. The notice on the door offers an out-of-hours service: 'To Motorists. When shop closed apply third door up the entry.' The advertising card, posted on 11 January 1911 to A.P. Brydson of Water Park, Greenodd, says: 'When the tyres arrive I shall put in hand at once and report to you.' The firm's cycle works were in Collin Croft and their advertising offered 'manufacturers and patentees of guns, cycles, fishing tackle, golf etc', as well as the motor business.

Tramways were built in both Carlisle and Barrow-in-Furness. The top picture shows Carlisle electric tram no. 9 in a cobbled English Street. Miss Tait's 'Family & Commercial' Victoria Hotel can be seen on the right. The system was powered from the Corporation's Electric Light and Power Station at James Street. In the lower picture is one of the early Barrow trams, which were towed, from 1884 to 1904, by a steam traction unit until that system too was electrified.

Road workers come in different forms. Here state-of-the-art technology can be seen laying concrete on the Heversham bypass, 1927. When contractors Monk and Co. had finished, the road was officially opened by the Prince of Wales and was known thereafter as 'The Prince's Way'. Below, the lone figure of the roadman – the length man – can be seen in the Stengal photograph of c. 1900, looking after his section of road at Jesus Church, Troutbeck, Windermere. The verges were neatly cut and the waste taken away on the wheelbarrow.

The days of the horse-drawn charabanc were numbered even as the next series of photographs were being taken. This is the scene in Newlands, near Keswick, at the 'Devil's Elbow' on the famous round coach trip through Borrowdale, over Honister to Buttermere, over to Newlands and back to Keswick. 'Mr Baddeley roundly asserts that Scotland and Ireland have nothing to equal it,' said *Pearson's Guide*, describing 'the finest circular excursion from Keswick – whatever else the visitor to Keswick may do he should certainly not miss this.'

Two other views of coaching in the Keswick area. Above, Abraham's picture of the morning gathering at the Keswick Hotel, 4 June 1912. These coaches took visitors on the four trips (or rounds) which every season kept coachmen and horses busy. Below, Pettitt's show a Riggs' coach climbing the Windermere road out of Keswick on the service route to Ambleside and Windermere (see also page 4).

*A Char-a-banc taking a difficult curve,*
*Is an excellent test of the passengers "nerve"*

'Touring in Lakeland' is the title of a humorous card from Valentine's of Dundee. Comparison with the photograph on page 73 reveals the likely location of the 'difficult curve'. This type of postcard – see also pages 20, 99 and 107 – was sent home by the thousand by visitors, but many considered that the wrong image of the Lake District was being projected.

A coachman stands by his charges at the Old England Hotel, Bowness-on-Windermere. Many hotels such as the Old England ran their own coach and charabanc tours as part of a week-long package holiday. Some hotels, such as the Taylor's Salutation at Ambleside, ran a coach company along with the hotel business and advertised their tours in the district around other hotels.

John Ellwood's carrier's cart pictured at Ayside near Newby Bridge, 1904. The service was from the Rose and Crown at Ulverston to the New Inn, Kendal via Cartmel and Grange-over-Sands, on Wednesdays and Saturdays. The Ellwoods were from Low Fell Yeat, Staveley and Black Beck Hall, Ayside. William Ridding, also of Ayside, was their carter.

# ULLSWATER (Royal Mail) SERVICE.

## PIONEERS OF THE DIRECT MOTOR SERVICE BETWEEN
# PENRITH AND PATTERDALE
### ALL THE YEAR ROUND.

This advertisement was for the motorized Royal Mail service, an early post bus, on Ullswaterside. George Taylor and Company worked from the Cumberland Garage, Penrith. Times were already changing, in the aftermath of the First World War. In an early 1920s guide Burrows stated: 'The motor traffic on the main roads of the Lake District during the season is very great.' The problem was allowed to grow until now the mixed planning system cannot find an answer.

A private motor bus service which ran for many years from Bowness to Windermere was C. Head's 'Magnet Bus'. The business from Windermere railway station to Bowness steamer pier was always lucrative during the season. This bus is waiting at Bowness pier.

Thomas John Coward was the foreman platelayer on the Furness Railway, Foxfield to Coniston branch line during the first decades of the twentieth century. Here he is photographed at Dalton Road Crossing at Torver. Thomas Wilson was the stationmaster at Torver station at this time. Related to the large family group of Newbys and Cowards in the Broughton to Coniston area Tom Coward's relations could be found on farms, in post offices and inns, joiners' shops and quarries. He also ran a smallholding to supplement his railway pay.

# MARKETS AND SHOPS

*John Fairer at the door of his
drapery shop at Verdun House,
Shap, 1905. He advertised as draper
and milliner at premises where four
generations of the family traded, in
tea as well as drapery, from 1855
until 1981.*

Two pictures of Carlisle street markets, late nineteenth century. The busy street scenes associated with the street trading were typical of the times. Note the umbrellas being used as parasols against the sun among the fruit and vegetable stalls in the lower picture. Carlisle market-days were Wednesdays and Saturdays.

Maryport and Whitehaven markets were photographed by Valentines of Dundee, c. 1903. The Maryport market, seen above with its neat row of open carts and smaller crowd, contrasts with the Whitehaven picture below, where the row of carts can be seen on the right, but very mixed in with the other dealers. Maryport market-day was Friday, and Whitehaven's were Tuesdays, Thursdays and Saturdays, with Thursday being the principal day.

Appleby market-day, *c*. 1910. Carts line up where cars park today and in the background the crowds gather round the market hall entrance and the stalls towards the cloisters. Appleby market-day was Saturday, and was 'well provided with corn and provisions', said the *Kelly's Directory* of the period, when Joseph Thomas Alderson of 4 Court, Burrowgate, was the market inspector and toll collector for Appleby Borough Corporation. Alderson was also school attendance officer and Town Hall caretaker.

Penrith market, pictured by Reeds in a later period, probably the early 1950s. In recent decades this part of Corn Market has changed with the provision of a market shelter. Note the horse and cart on the left – a rare survivor by that time. Market-day in Penrith was (and is) on Tuesday.

New Market Street, Ulverston, on market-day, late 1940s. The 'No Waiting' sign indicates another age. The crowds on the right gather round the outdoor stalls at the top of New Market Street and along to the Market Hall. New Market Street and its market hall took much of Ulverston market out of the Market Place and King Street. Ulverston market-day is Thursday.

Keswick market photographed by Maysons of Keswick, 1920s. John W. Edgar of Workington's fruit and vegetable stall stands out among the unmarked stalls. Car parking has now been allowed to intrude on the centre of Keswick although the weekly reminder of the town's beginnings manages to survive. Keswick market-day is Saturday.

Satterthwaite's fruit stall, inside the original market hall in Ulverston. The first market hall was built 'in the Italian style of architecture' in 1875 and burned down in 1935, when it was replaced with the market hall we see today. William Satterthwaite, 'wholesale and retail fish and fruit salesman' at 11 Market Hall, lived at 34 Hill Fall, Ulverston.

An outdoor market of a different sort was the daily display outside 'Fenty' Robinson's main shop on Crag Brow at Bowness-on-Windermere. He had another shop underneath the Chestnut Tree on the other side of the road. Frank Robinson's fent dealer's (fabrics) shop was a Bowness institution, from its opening in 1887 to its closure in 1959. In the early days this was also a servants' registry for the benefit of all the big houses. Frank Robinson also collected old pictures which drew many to see his albums, and these are now preserved in the Windermere Library.

The Broom Inn at Blackpoolgate, Bewcastle, was in the wild triangle of Cumberland bordering Scotland and Northumberland, a very remote location. John Waugh, the licensee, and his wife and dog pose for the photographer. At the turn of the century William Armstrong had this licence. The inn catered for a widely scattered population.

Beaty's shop at 2 English Street, Longtown. The business started in the mid-nineteenth century as a combined drapery and grocery shop owned by William and George Beaty, but by 1901 they advertised as drapers and tailors. By the 1920s the business had the name William and John Beaty.

Robinson Brothers' Brewery in the Gill and Brook Street, Ulverston, advertised themselves as 'Brewers of superior ginger ale in stone bottles – an excellent summer beverage. Agent for Bass & Co pale and mild Burton Ales.' The turn of the century picture is by W. Holmes of Ulverston.

R.W. and T.K. Thompson's shop on the corner of Finkle Street and Branthwaite Brow, Kendal (42/44 Finkle Street was the address). They advertised as outfitters, hatters, hosiers, shirt and glove warehouse and gents' mercers. In 1910 Robert William Thompson lived at Town View, and Thomas Kitching Thompson lived at Hillside. Their business, started in the mid-nineteenth century, lasted until the mid-twentieth.

Robert T. Dixon of Yard 123, Highgate, is claimed to be Kendal's last hand-loom weaver. Kendal wool and Kendal weaving were the source of much of the town's past prosperity. Here, pictured just after the First World War, Dixon can be seen with his primitive hand-loom. Wool weaving in Kendal now is limited to the manufacture of carpets.

# JOSEPH TAYLOR,

## Brush Manufacturer, KING STREET, ULVERSTON.

Joseph Taylor, brush manufacturer of Ulverston, used this large illustrated advertisement in 1901 to show off his manufacture of brushes, laundry hampers, clothes baskets, dolly tubs, dolly legs, mats, cocoa matting, cradles, baskets, cords, twines, cooperage, wash leathers, sponges, combs, and more. Working from premises at 26 and 30 King Street, Joseph Taylor, who lived at 7 Hoad Terrace, also had the Ure Mill and 18 Market Street for his large and varied business.

Thomas Swainson of the Elleray Hotel ran a wholesale ale and porter bottling business at Cross and Victoria Streets, Windermere, seen here *c.* 1905. The picture shows the Windermere Bottling Stores with the barrels being delivered and the bottles going out in crates. Founded in 1874 as an 'Aerated and Mineral Water Manufacturers' Swainsons supplied the great demand from the holiday hotels, bars and catering establishments for both alcoholic and non-alcoholic refreshment.

Mawson and Partners, 'nursery men and landscape gardeners', had what would now be called their 'garden centre' photographed by Atkinson and Pollitt in April 1934. Having been famous garden designers for the big houses, Mawsons entered the popular market as times changed. 'Call Lakeland Nurseries, New Road. Tel: Windermere 44.'

Coal was until fairly recently the most widely used fuel, with peat and logs a close second in rural areas. Above, George Dawson delivers coal to Joe Bland's premises in Gandy Street for the coal merchant James Waldie of Station Yard, Kendal, 1950. Below, Walter Latham of 5 Lynnslack Terrace, Arnside, loads coal on to a motor lorry at the Arnside railway station goods siding, *c.* 1940. Hard, dirty work for both.

W. Rigg had a fruiterer's business in Grasmere at the turn of the century and also offered a delivery service to farms and houses in the district. Here he can be seen on his rounds in about 1905 on what must have been a chilly day as both he and the horse have a coat on. Many traders had extensive delivery services to their outlying customers.

Ambleside butcher William Hoban acquired his own shop and also had a delivery service in the 1930s, after starting with butcher Thomas Machell Dixon on Compston Road in the 1920s. One of his early vehicles was this three-wheel van, reg. no. JM 749. William's mother-in-law was Mary Fell (née Pepper) from Holme Ground, Tilberthwaite.

Visiting the shop at Tilberthwaite Farm was not very easy when Budge occupied the wicker chair in the gate. One must wonder how many decided not to try. Mary Fell, the mother of Bill Hoban's wife Dorothy (in the previous picture), lived here before moving to Holme Ground Farm across the valley. This tenanted farm was not only a place to call for refreshments, it was also one of the centres for the Langdale linen industry started by Mary's grandmother.

The Co-operative Movement spread throughout the Lake Counties, and many small societies were formed. The Ulverston Co-operative Society Bakery delivery van is seen here, decorated for the hospital parade, c. 1935. On the left stands Harry Goldstraw with his brother-in-law, Co-op employee Joseph William Kitchin. Both had married Coward girls from Foxfield. Both Harry and Joseph served throughout the First World War among the horrors of the trenches and had little to say about it afterwards. Joseph was chief bell-ringer at Ulverston Parish Church for many decades.

The employees of the Kirkby Ireleth Co-operative Society Ltd pose here, 1911. Standing (left to right): Miss D. Tyson (drapery), Mr I. Gaskell (warehouse), Miss Tyson (manageress of drapery), Mr F. Tyson (boots). Seated: Mr J. Hartley (boots), Mr G. Armistead (grocery), Mr Henry Briggs (general manager), Mr H. Coward (manager of boots), Mr G. Barr (grocery), Mr R. Tyson (grocery).

Herbert Bland of 13, 15, 17 and 19 New Shambles, Kendal, used this postcard as a tradecard to introduce clients to his tailoring business in the 1930s. In this time of economic depression Herbert's trade in bespoke tailoring using a number of tailors must have been very difficult.

Section Five

# THE HOLIDAY 'INDUSTRY'

*Motor charabancs mingle with horse charabancs as the revolution in transport got under way at the time of the First World War. The charabancs wait at Penrith railway station for the arrival of trip trains full of London and North Western Railway tourists.*

William Wilson at the 'Tourists' Rest' hut at Easedale, Grasmere, photographed by the famous Lakeland photographer Herbert Bell of Ambleside. It is reported that William offered guided tours and mountain climbing lessons, and he also sold refreshments from this hut built against a large boulder on the side of Easedale Tarn.

Mrs Ada Honey, the proprietress of the Seatoller House, Borrowdale, photographed by G.P. Abraham of Keswick. The house was that of the Honister quarry manager Moses Pepper (who came from Kirkby-in-Furness with its huge slate quarries). Mrs Mary Jane Pepper, his wife, made the premises famous as a Lakeland boarding house with, for example, Sir Charles Trevelyan taking twenty to twenty-five people there every Whitsuntide for more than thirty-five years. Mary's daughters assisted her in her later years (she died at eighty-five) and her daughter Ada (by then Mrs Honey) continued for many years after Mary Jane's death. A brother of Moses, Robert Pepper, married Elizabeth Heskett of Langdale and went to live at Holme Ground, Tilberthwaite, in May 1888.

Green Grove, Gilsland, in the far north of Cumberland on the Northumberland border, was also in the accommodation business. Many tourists came to visit the Roman wall and the then famous and fashionable spa. In an 1897 directory accommodation at Green Grove was offered by James Hope, James Smith and William Storrow.

The Lodore Hotel at Borrowdale was built to replace a humbler establishment. The site was famous for its waterfall, which very often had no water, and the Borrowdale echo, which resulted from the firing of a cannon. The new hotel is seen here in the early twentieth century. Its original mid-nineteenth-century central section can be seen with the later additions erected on either side. This Maysons postcard was sent in 1915 to Mr McNeal of Pilling, asking: 'When you go to market on Saturday please leave 5/- of eggs with Mr. West, Bookseller, and oblige. – Thos Percy.'

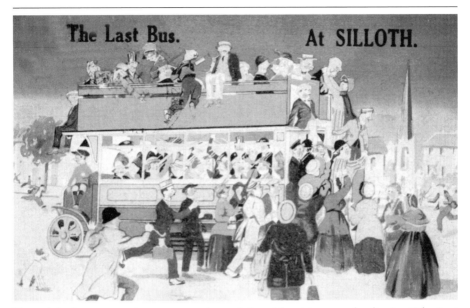

The Last Bus. At SILLOTH.

Two of the humorous picture postcards much loved by visitors to the district. 'The Last Bus at Silloth' is an E.T.W. Dennis production of the 1920s which scoffs at the overcrowded public transport. Below, the earlier Cynicus postcard digs at the accommodation in peaceful Ulverston: 'For a quiet retreat it can't be beat!'

For a quiet retreat it can't be beat!
Come and join us at
Ulverston

The Romney Hotel at Ambleside, early 1950s. It is of interest in a collection such as this to include memories of hotels which are no more. The terrace of the Romney Hotel at Waterhead was a busy scene which will never be seen again, as the hotel has recently been demolished to make way for flats.

The Furness Abbey Hotel is also no more. It was part of the Furness Railway holiday industry and was built on the site, and included part, of the medieval Furness Abbey's outbuildings. Here the porter can be seen walking a visitor's terriers in front of the medieval arch that at one time was the gate to the abbey precinct. The picture is from the Raphael Tuck postcard series for the railway, produced around 1910.

Two views of the Ferry Hotel on Windermere lake. The first is by Brunskills of Windermere, *c*. 1902. Taken from the steamer pier, it shows the hotel in its Edwardian heyday. The view was sent to Miss S. Vickers of Hammerbank as a birthday card on 9 December 1905. The picture below is from the 'Duplex Album' series published for the hotel by the RAP Co. in book form in the 1930s. It shows the staircase lounge of the hotel furnished very much in the style of the period. The building has been a laboratory for many years now.

Thompson's Tea Rooms at Pooley Bridge were photographed by S.M. Gibson and Co. before the First World War. Written on the back of the picture is: 'Misses Thompson, Pooley Bridge, July 17 & 18th. Supper, bedroom, breakfast etc 8/6d.' The sign offers 'Pleasure Boats and Yachts, Accommodation, Cyclists'.

The Commercial Hotel at Kendal (now also no more) advertised as the headquarters of the Cyclists Touring Club when Mrs A. Hoggarth was the proprietress in about 1905. The hotel omnibus which collected visitors from the railway station stands ready at the door, with the hotel porter and boots waiting for clients. This once-important hotel was renamed The Kendal Hotel in its latter years, but the building now houses a branch of a building society.

The pergola at The Swan Hotel at Newby Bridge, on the side of the River Leven as it leaves Windermere. This was a great turn-of-the-century attraction to visitors to the hotel. The picture was taken by Sankeys of Barrow in the first decade of the twentieth century, purchased from the hotel on a visit there in 1926 and used as a postcard in March 1966. It took more than fifty years to travel from photographer to postman.

A café for the day-trip visitor was the Park Hotel Café in Station Road, Keswick, photographed by Maysons, 1920s. When the railway reached Keswick visitors started arriving in their thousands, many only for the day, and the Park Hotel in Station Road, near the railway station, offered an obvious answer to refreshment problems. Previously Thomas Martin had offered accommodation at the Park Temperance Hotel which would attract many of those who visited the annual religious convention.

Visitors to Grange-over-Sands arriving by the boatload from Morecambe, c. 1905. G. Wilson from Grange went down on the sands to photograph the prawner yachts, many built by Crosfields of Arnside, being used as holiday boats instead of the usual fishing trade. Many residents of Grange deeply resented the activities of the boatmen, the railways and the coach proprietors for bringing visitors, and the hoteliers and café owners for providing accommodation and refreshment for them.

The Bowness Bay Boating Association's registered office at R. Blaylock's boathouse was against the railway company pier at Bowness-on-Windermere in the 1930s. The association was very protective of its trading rights in boating on the lake. At the time, as well as Blaylocks, Bowness Bay boat hirers were J. Atkinson, Borwicks, J. Campbell, H. Dixon, J. Hodgson, S. Lee, J. Robinson, W. Robinson, N. Shepherd, G.N. Suart, T. Storey, J. Tebay, B. Waters and the Bowness Bay Motor Launch Company. New 'boats for hire' owners were *not* welcome.

The Steamer Pier at Waterhead, Ambleside, just before the LMS Railway took over the boat ownership from the Furness Railway, 1920s. An overcrowded boat and a busy pier indicate a good day for company. The rights for the conveyance of passengers from Newby Bridge (later Lakeside) to Bowness and Ambleside by steamer was much fought over during the nineteenth century but was consolidated under Furness Railway ownership. This later passed to the LMS Railway and then British Rail. Modern times have seen the service returned to private hands, with large motor-boats competing but not able to use the piers.

The Furness Railway also ran paddle-steamers across Morecambe Bay to Fleetwood before the First World War. The Blackpool visitor was offered a packaged day-trip to Barrow and on to Windermere or Coniston by train, and even charabanc trips into the central lakes area. Some only went to Furness Abbey and to see Romney's house at Dalton, but full facilities were provided by the Furness Railway throughout. Hardworking Sankeys of Barrow took pictures on most trips to sell on the return journey. Here on 1 August 1910 the *Lady Moyra* ploughs across the bay with members of the crew assisting passengers. Note the boy with the sweet basket, bottom left.

# The Last Boat
# Ambleside to Bowness

Cynicus of Tayport strikes again, this time to criticize the overcrowded lake steamers on Windermere at the end of the nineteenth century (see also page 99). The 'Last Boat from Ambleside to Bowness' would strike a chord with many lake users, as overcrowding was common – see the pictures opposite. Posted on 16 August 1910 the message reads: 'We are on a tour here today the weather is grand – wish you were with us.'

The crowds were not so large for 'A Busy Day at Arnside', photographed by J.D. Wilson of Arnside in his Lilyland series, c. 1910. Visitors were conveyed in rowing boats to the larger prawner yachts for a trip around Morecambe Bay. The ports of Sandside and Arnside were once the only ports in Westmorland, but the building of the railway in 1857 stopped their trade.

The *Teal* was originally put together at Vickers' Works at Barrow, then taken apart and conveyed by railway to Lakeside where the parts were reassembled, and fitting out took place before her launch in 1936. The reassembly is complete and fitting out under way in this picture. The new *Teal* replaced a steamer built in 1879. In 1938 the new *Swan* was built in the same way, to replace an older boat launched in 1869. The old boats were then scrapped. The 1930s *Swan* and *Teal* are both still working the lake today but in a much altered form.

*Section Six*

# SERVING THE PUBLIC

*The Westmorland County Council main switch-board at County Hall, Kendal, with Mrs Abigail Lizzie Heskett Reed in charge, October 1967. She was for many years 'the voice of the county council'. Abigail's family were the Heskett/Pepper family from Tilberthwaite, Coniston. Westmorland County Council ceased to exist on 1 April 1974 and their county hall is now just offices and meeting rooms used by Cumbria County Council.*

The Tan Hill Inn is above Barras, Kirkby Stephen, Westmorland and Keld in Swaledale in Yorkshire but is in fact in County Durham. The boundaries of all three counties came together near here. The postman stands at the road junction to Barras and Keld and is in Yorkshire, but the snow-covered background is shared with Westmorland and Durham. The inn is a left-over from the days when the moors all round were worked for coal and it claims to be the highest inn in England. There was virtually no local population but it managed to survive on a publicized reputation for its height above sea level (1,732 ft) and an unpublicized reputation for its total disregard for licensing hours, until the motor car allowed easier access. Its survival is even stranger in an area which was then well known for strict temperance movements.

Calder Bridge post office photographed by Brittain and Wright of Stockton when Joseph Geldart was postmaster, *c.* 1900. The Geldarts were farmers, joiners, cartwrights and saw- and corn-mill proprietors, and William Geldart was a parish councillor. The post arrived at 8.30 a.m. and was despatched at 4.40 p.m. On Sundays there was no despatch but the telegraph was open from 8 a.m. to 10 a.m.

Two Salvation Army workers in Maryport pose for the Hesket Andrews Photographic Art Studio at 108 Senhouse Street, Maryport, late nineteenth century. The Salvation Army Barracks was in John Street, where in 1897 William E. Hough was captain with his barracks open from 11 a.m. to 6.30 p.m. and 8 p.m. 'every evening'. Their unique blend of military discipline and religion helped many of the poor and deprived in the then busy working seaport town.

Mr George Newby of Thompstead, Woodland, poses with his wife for photographer S. Jeavons of 9 Paxton Street, Barrow-in-Furness, 1906. He had completed thirty years as parish clerk, and was also the sexton, grave-digger and bellringer at Woodland Church. He was also reputed to have dug nearly all the graves in the churchyard since its consecration in 1865. Starting as a farm servant and then a farmer he subsequently took to working in the woods, becoming much in demand as a master at wood fencing. In 1901 his large garden was described as 'a pattern of neatness', and George as 'wiry, hard as nails and an early riser'. The Revd James Park was the rector at Woodland when Mackereths of Ulverston commissioned the photograph.

This picture is by R. Henderson, the chemist of Station Street, Keswick. It shows the sexton at work in the burial ground at Crosthwaite Church when Hardwicke Drummond Rawnsley was the vicar. Canon Rawnsley, a friend of John Ruskin and Beatrix Potter, became famous as a founder of the National Trust. He raised a number of Lakeland memorials (see page 126).

The pupils at Old College, Windermere, with Mr and Mrs Ferreira, work hard on making a footpath at the school. This is another photograph from the 1920s prospectus (see also page 24), which obviously offered character-building hard work to the benefit of the school's owners. Arthur Hamilton Raikes MA (Oxon), JP, was headmaster and Captain Henry Martin Ferreira, ex-Flight Commander RAF, Croix de Guerre and Star was joint principal, 'preparing a limited number of gentlemen's sons, aged seven to fourteen, for the Public Schools and the Royal Navy'.

Stramongate School, Kendal, was founded as a Quaker school in 1698, and the famous scientist John Dalton was at one time a teacher there. In the early 1900s the school had become quite famous as a boarding and preparatory school, where, 'with a laboratory, for science, gymnasium, workshop, darkroom, cycle house, etc many eminent men have been educated'.

The Windermere Sea Scouts was one of the first troops in the country, and was founded by J. Mortimer Sladen, a friend of Lord Baden-Powell. The outbreak of the First World War saw them using their skills in the defence of their country. In November 1914 they were sent to Saltburn and Whitby on the east coast where they acted as look-outs and coastguards against the enemy. Here they are seen on duty with a sailor companion, at work a long way from home.

The inspection of the Cumberland and Westmorland Constabulary guard of honour at Keswick railway station on 17 October 1956. The Queen walks with Superintendent Nixon of Whitehaven, with Mr Watson the chief constable behind. The policemen on parade had many war medals on display, a number of them having had a distinguished wartime career in the forces. What would they think of today? (The same location decades earlier can be seen on page 74.)

The Kendal volunteer fire brigade pose with their horse-drawn hand-pump fire engine at the back of Stricklandgate House, Kendal, 1890s. They were shortly to move to new premises on Aynam Road. Members of the borough watch committee and the police, who ran the brigade, pose for photographer James Henry Hogg of 71 Stricklandgate, himself a one-time borough councillor and watch committee member.

Workington Red Cross nurses pose for the camera of Debenhams of 158 Pow Street, Workington, at a rally in Lowther Park about the time of the First World War. Volunteer nursing groups such as this were as important to the government's plans as volunteer soldiers.

The interior of the new operating theatre at the Cottage Hospital in Ulverston, installed in 1904, was photographed for Mackereth's *1905 Year Book*. The architect was J.W. Grundy of Brogden Street. Originally built in 1872 the hospital was supported mainly by the Annual Hospital Parade Committee. After Grundy's alterations it was said: 'This establishment is now replete with every modern appliance for the successful treatment of suffering humanity.'

The Ethel Hedley Orthopaedic Hospital for Children, Troutbeck Bridge, Windermere, 1920s. Once the property of the Watson family, Calgarth Park was built as a replacement for the ancient Calgarth Hall. The building was used by the government during the First World War as a hospital for wounded soldiers and is now flats. This picture was taken by Octavius C. Wilmot of Ambleside.

The Blencathra Sanatorium on the side of the mountain of that name near Keswick is now a centre for outdoor studies. It was being run by 'The Cumberland Branch of the National Association for the Prevention of Consumption and Other Forms of Tuberculosis' when Pettitts of Keswick photographed it just after the First World War. Built in 1904 to provide fresh-air treatment for consumptive patients, the sanatorium closed when antibiotics were discovered to cure TB.

Arthur Roden poses with his daughter for a photograph which was used as a Christmas card, c. 1905. Mr and Mrs Roden started trading in the holiday apartments business at Crown Villa, Windermere, but then moved to the West End House where this stiffly posed picture was taken.

Military service was part of life for many in the first decades of the twentieth century. In the top picture, Kendal Volunteers wait outside the Kendal Drill Hall to go off to the First World War, 1914. In the lower picture, other volunteers from Lancashire attend one of the pre-war annual training camps at Holmescales, near Kendal, August 1911. The lads are stuffing empty palliasse and pillow covers with hay to provide the unit with beds.

The arrival of the artillery at the Burton and Holme railway station of the London and North Western Railway line on 14 October 1912 again illustrates pre-war training for the horrors to come. The lower picture shows soldiers from the north-east in camp at Greystoke, near Penrith, also in 1914. The 'pals' battalions of Kitchener's army were raised by rousing recruiting speeches and newspaper articles. The nation was shocked by the high casualty figures among the volunteers who went off to this war.

## Section Seven

# SOME WATER WORKS

*The diver at work in the nineteenth century in
Barrow docks, with an Irish or Isle of Man
paddle steamer being worked on in the background. This was dangerous work for the diver
in dirty water. Both the Furness Railway and
the shipbuilding company employed divers.*

Net fishing at Ulverston, 1898. Mr J. Eastwood won the 5s prize in Mackereth's photo competition with this picture of the local fishermen with their nets. Working between the tides the fishermen waited for the return of the sea and the fish it carried into their nets. Some netted fish from boats, others used stakes to suspend the net across the channel. Fluke fishing also sustained many local families through hard times.

The *Gladys* of Liverpool, a small steamer coaster, waits at Ulverston canal foot pier for the tide. The picture from the first decade of the twentieth century is by James Atkinson of Ulverston. Ulverston Canal was completed in 1796 but the opening of a port at Barrow brought about its decline. The canal was sealed off from the sea in 1949 to make a fresh-water reservoir for Glaxo whose factory had been built on the ironworks site.

The launch of the Australian Commonwealth liner *Jervis Bay* was photographed by Sankeys, the official photographers for Vickers, the Barrow shipbuilder, 17 January 1922. She was the last of three *Bay* liners for the Australian government. In 1939 *Jervis Bay* was taken over by the Admiralty as an armed merchant cruiser and her name went down in maritime history, as on 5 November 1940 she took on and was sunk by the Nazi battleship *Admiral Scheer*, thus saving the convoy she was escorting. Her captain was awarded a posthumous VC.

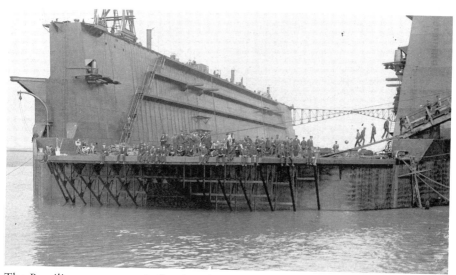

The Brazilian government's floating dock being put together in Walney Channel, Barrow-in-Furness, after being launched in three parts, June 1910. Again the picture is by the brilliant photographer Edward Sankey whose work must rank as the best in Cumbria, recording, as it does among much else, the industrial activity in the Barrow area around the turn of the century.

Cockling at Grange-over-Sands pictured by local photographer Hankinson, *c.* 1912.
Rocking a 'jumbo' on the sand and digging out the cockles with a three-pronged fork
called a 'cram' was a way of life with the fishing families from this coast. The railway in
the background improved the market for these fisherfolk who used it to get their
catches of mussels, cockles and flukes to the towns and cities of Britain. Modern
pollution has changed much in this bay.

A coaster, probably the *Stainburn*, owned by Henry Reynolds of Whitehaven, leaves
Workington harbour probably laden with coal for Ireland, 1920s. Note the bucket
dredger in the background.

Senhouse dock at Maryport in its heyday – a busy scene with steam and sail mixed together. When the Elizabeth dock, built in 1857, proved too small for the increased trade and size of shipping, a new larger dock, almost twice the size, was constructed, and this was opened by Mrs Senhouse on 27 May 1884. The whole town had a day's holiday and a commemorative medal was struck for the occasion. The photograph is by Valentines of Dundee.

*Bluebird II* arrives at Coniston in August 1939. Named by eighteen-year-old Donald Campbell, Sir Malcolm Campbell's 2,500 hp hydroplane speedboat was to break the speed record at 142 miles per hour on 19 August. There was originally opposition to the attempt by the Friends of the Lake District but this was withdrawn at the insistence of their chairman, Canon Wilcox, vicar of Coniston. The Friends of Brantwood continued to oppose speedboats using the lake. One man threatened to go fishing on the course. The twelve-cylinder Rolls-Royce Schneider Trophy engine was soon to be used in fighter aircraft, and Admiral du Cane of the Admiralty, who had designed the hull with Vosper, remarked that valuable lessons had been learned in motor torpedo-boat design. The Second World War started two weeks later on 3 September 1939.

Charles Gough, a Kendal Quaker, became the subject of much romantic legend when he died on Helvellyn in 1805. His dog remained with the body for three months, inspiring Sir Walter Scott and William Wordsworth to write about this unusual fidelity. When Miss Frances Power Cobbe suggested to Canon Hardwicke Rawnsley of Crosthwaite, Keswick, that 'some record of that heroic creature should be placed where passers-by might see and ponder', the canon, who helped found the National Trust in 1893/5, put the matter in hand. Two verses of Wordsworth's poem 'Fidelity' starting, 'The dog which still was hovering nigh, Repeating the same timid cry', were carved on a stone slab with a dedication and installed on Helvellyn in a specially erected cairn on 18 June 1891. Herbert Bell, the photographer from Ambleside, recorded the building of the cairn for posterity, with the worthy canon watching the masons at work.

# *Acknowledgements*

The production of this book would not have been possible without the assistance in many ways of the following: Mrs A. Barnet of Kendal, Mr W. Barrow, the Chief Constable of Cumbria, Mr G. Dawson, Mr J. Fairer of Shap, Mr H. Fancy, Whitehaven Museum, Mr J. Garbutt, Allithwaite, Mr I. Grey of Longtown, Mrs V. Grindrod of Tilberthwaite, Mrs K. Hayhurst of the Holme and District LHS, Mrs Hodgson of Little Langdale, Mrs H. Jones of Kendal, Mr C.H. Moss, Troutbeck Bridge, Mrs A. Reed of Kendal, Mrs B. Smith of Bewcastle, Mrs C. Strickland of the Kendal Library, Mrs M. Storey of Longtown, Mr and Mrs J. Story of Kendal, Mrs A.V. Thomas of Longtown, Mrs O. Wilson of Calgarth, and the many people who encourage and support me in my hobby of collecting photographic images of the past. I also wish to acknowledge those families of the county into which this book intrudes.

# BRITAIN IN OLD PHOTOGRAPHS

To order any of these titles please telephone Littlehampton Book Services on 01903 721596